HABIT CH

MASTER YOUR NEXT MOVE

Be One Step Ahead of The Life Game

Christopher Nash

Table of Contents

Chapter 1: The Power of Imperfect Starts 6

Chapter 2: 10 Habits You Must Stop If You Want To Manifest What You Want In Life 9

Chapter 3: How Luck Is Created From Success 14

Chapter 4: Fight Lethargy and Win 16

Chapter 5: Be Inspired to Create 20

Chapter 6: Why You Are Setting The Wrong Goals 22

Chapter 7: Doing The Thing You Love Most 26

Chapter 8: Fight Is The Reward 28

Chapter 9: Hitting Rock Bottom 31

Chapter 10: 10 Habits of Tiger Woods 35

Chapter 11: 10 Habits of Jeff Bezos 39

Chapter 12: Why You're Demotivated By Lack of Clarity 44

Chapter 13: Bounce Back From Failure 48

Chapter 14: How to Deal with Stress Head On? 7 Things You Can Start Today 51

Chapter 15: Being Mentally Strong 56

Chapter 16: How To Use Affirmations For Success 58

Chapter 17: 5 Ways Quitting Something Can Bring You Joy 60

Chapter 18: Stop Lying To Yourself 63

Chapter 19: 10 Habits For A Clean Home 66

Chapter 20: 10 Habits That Give Me Joy 74

Chapter 21: If You Commit to Nothing, You'll Be Distracted By Everything 79

Chapter 22: 10 Habits of Roger Federer 82

Chapter 23: 10 Habits of Larry Page 86

Chapter 24: *Your Motivational Partner In Life* 90

Chapter 25: 10 Ways To Build New Habits by Taking Advantage of Old Ones 93

Chapter 26: 10 Habits of Michael Phelps 97

Chapter 27: *Stop Ignoring Your Health* 101

Chapter 28: *Motivation With Good Feelings* 104

Chapter 29: How to Value Being Alone 107

Chapter 30: 10 Habits of Novak Djokovic 110

Chapter 31: 8 Habits That Make People Dislike You 114

Chapter 32: How To Set Smart Goals 119

Chapter 33: How To Crush Your Goals This Quarter 122

Chapter 34: How Not To Waste Your 25,000 Mornings As An Adult. 125

Chapter 1:

The Power of Imperfect Starts

When you have a goal — starting a business or eating healthier, or traveling the world — it's easy to look at someone who is already doing it and then try to reverse engineer their strategy. In some cases, this is useful. Learning from the experiences of successful people is a great way to accelerate your learning curve.

But it's equally important to remember that the systems, habits, and strategies that successful people are using today are probably not the same ones they were using when they began their journey. What is optimal for them right now isn't necessarily needed for you to get started. There is a difference between the two.

Let me explain.

What is Optimal vs. What is Needed

Learning from others is great, and I do it all the time myself.

But comparing your current situation to someone already successful can often make you feel like you lack the required resources to get started at all. If you look at their optimal setup, it can be really easy to convince yourself that you need to buy new things or learn new skills or meet new people before you can even take the first step toward your goals.

And usually, that's not true. Here are two examples.

Starting a business. When you're an entrepreneur, it's so easy to get obsessed with optimal. This is especially true at the start. I can remember being convinced that my first website would not succeed without a great logo. After all, every popular website I looked at had a professional logo. I've since learned my lesson. Now my "logo" is just my name, and this is the most popular website I've built.

Eating healthy. Maybe the optimal diet would involve buying beef that is only grass-fed or vegetables that are only organic, or some other super-healthy food strategy. But if you're just trying to make strides in the right direction, why get bogged down in the details? Start small and simply buy another vegetable this week — whether it's organic or not. There will be plenty of time for optimization later.

Avoiding by Optimizing

Claiming that you need to "learn more" or "get all of your ducks in a row" can often be a crutch that prevents you from moving forward on the stuff that matters.

- You can complain that your golf game is suffering because you need new clubs, but the truth is you probably just need two years of practice.

- You can point out how your business mentor is successful because they use XYZ software, but they probably got started without it.

Obsessing about the ultimate strategy, diet, or golf club can be a clever way to prevent yourself from doing hard work.

An imperfect start can always be improved, but obsessing over a perfect plan will never take you anywhere on its own.

Chapter 2:

<u>10 Habits You Must Stop If You Want To Manifest What You Want In Life</u>

We all have our deep secret desires of what we would want to turn into buried in our hearts. We hardly say it aloud lest we are judged harshly by an ungrateful society. It is ungrateful because the same society that celebrates when you in your win shall bash you when you slip.

You may have tried out very many things to bring to life your not-so-alive wishes but your efforts have been in vain. Here are ten things that you must stop if you want to manifest what you want in life:

1. <u>Trusting Everhbody</u>

You may have heard of an old saying that you should keep your friends close and your enemies even closer. This is true especially when you are about to make a major move. Open trust is often violated and you will suffer a series of heartbreaks if you do not cease handing people your trust on a platter.

Trust is earned. Let your friends earn it by continuously proving their loyalty and friendship to you. If you give the wrong people your trust, they will stand in your way of manifesting what you want in life. They will poison your dreams and before you know it, you have lost it all.

2. <u>Sharing yYour Plans Openly</u>

It is not everybody who has your best interest at heart. Some people close to you could be orchestrating your downfall and the more information you reveal the easier it is to bring you down. Be unpredictable if you want to manifest what you want in life.

Manifestation requires some degree of secrecy. Work in silence and let your success introduce you. Stop being an open book for others to read. What could be an innocent act of honesty can turn the tables against you and hinder manifestation.

3. Procrastination

To procrastinate is to postpone action to a later time without proper reason. Sometimes an idea would strike your mind and instead of implementing it immediately, you decide to wait to act after some time. This will make you lose sight of what you wanted to do.

Procrastination kills unborn dreams and is an enemy to your progress. Strike the rod when it is hot. You can consult with people you trust before taking a concrete decision after which you must not delay implementing it.

4. Taking Issues Lightly

There is a big problem when you consider everything at face value. There is always more than what meets the eye. Stop assuming what people say on something concerning you and investigate their motive. This is how you will sift genuine friends from fake ones.

Question the obvious if you have any doubt. This will make you have clarity of mind to make sober decisions. Manifestation requires sobriety.

What you overlook or assume could make a great difference in decision-making.

5. Blaming Other People

Great people do not play the blame game. Instead, they innovate solutions to existing problems. They are proactive in society and this makes them stand out in a highly polarized environment.

Stop blaming people for your woes, real or perceived, and work towards not falling into the same trap again. Excuses stand in the way of the manifestation of your dreams. Do not cry foul every time things go wrong. Choose to make them right and chart your way forward. Two wrongs do not make a right.

6. Allowing Other People To Make Deciison On Your Behalf

Why should someone else make decisions for you while you are not incapacitated? They could be biased to your dreams and make key decisions out of line with your goals. Stop giving them the mandate to run your life, do it yourself.

It is right to accept advice and heed it but it does not mean that your advisors should make decisions for you. You choose whether or not to heed the advice. The ultimate responsibility of decision-making rests with you.

7. Casting aspersions On Your Ability

You should not doubt your ability or competence; when you do, nobody will believe you. Self-doubt gives other people the license to demean and underestimate your ability. Manifestation requires self-confidence on your part.

In his book, *the 48 laws of power*, Robert Greene writes that you should enter action with boldness. Conversely, you sign your death warranty when you timidly shy away from challenges thrown your way.

8. Disrespecting Authority

Rebellion to authorities is a sign of weakness and bad character. Respect authority from the family to the national level because they are in place to bring equality and level the playing field for its people from all races and backgrounds.

How can you expect manifestation for what you want in life when you are rebellious to the same authority supposed to take care of you? You will similarly be disrespected when you are in a position of power.

9. Being Pessimistic

Pessimism has closed potential doors of breakthrough for many people. It crushes any hope of success left. To succeed in what you do, you need to take the initiative despite the odds being against you. You will not see anything good when you are pessimistic.

A pessimistic mind is an enemy of progress. It makes you your own worst enemy. Remove this barrier and start thinking positively and you will make great gains in life.

10. Making A Comparison Of Your Life With Others

Life does not come with a manual. Everybody has their question paper to tackle. You therefore cannot copy from anyone else. It is disastrous when you copy the lifestyle of somebody else. You lose your identity when you judge yourself by another person's standards.

Your success is different from your neighbors'. Be encouraged when you clap for other people until your turn arrives. Stop judging yourself harshly if you have not won like your neighbor. Celebrate with them as you count the blessings at your doorstep.

In conclusion, it is agreeable that there are bad habits we ought to stop if we want to manifest what we want in life. These ten habits shed light on a dozen others that we need to stop to achieve manifestation.

Chapter 3:

How Luck Is Created From Success

Success and luck, just two simple words with meaning more profound than the ocean. These words are interrelated. For everyone, success has a different meaning because everyone has a distant dream to fulfill. Some people want a simple life, but some want to live with the luxuries of life. "Dream big" we all have heard this; setting high goals for the future proves that you believe in yourself, that you can do it after it is only you that can make you a success. Some people believe in luck, but luck goes hand in hand with hard work, determination, creativity. To earn the victory, you will always have to work hard, and you can't just leave everything on luck. But how can you make your luck from success? One may ask.

There are a few simple steps to make your luck. When you face a failure, don't just give up yet, don't ever assume that you can't do anything about the situation. It would be best if you decided to take control. It would help if you believed that you could handle the situation and fix the problems; when has giving up ever been suitable for someone's life. When you decide to take control of things, things turn out to be just fine.

As I said before, believing in yourself is a significant part of making your luck. Do something now. Stop postponing things you want to do, gather some willpower, and do it now before it's too late. Another thing you can do to learn to be lucky is to sit back and make a list of various options; if you can't follow up on one of the options, then go for the other one. Think about as many options as you can; just be creative.

When something holds us back, it is tough for us to move forward, or when you are stuck at the same routine and are not doing anything to move forward, luck can do nothing about your laziness. Take out time for yourself and decide about how you will move forward, how you will grow. Consider every single alternative out there. After determining what you want to do in the future, seek the opportunities. Whenever you think you have a chance, take action; now is not the time to sit back and watch; it is the time to run and grab that opportunity because you never know when the next time will come.

Successful people are committed to the fact that they want to be in control of their lives; that is how you make your luck from your success. It's all about believing in yourself.

Chapter 4:

Fight Lethargy and Win

Life is a continuous grind. Life is the summation of our efforts. Life is series of things that no one thinks can happen. But they do, and they do for a reason. Your life is no different than anyone else. You have the same needs and somewhat the same goals. But you might still be a failure while the world moves on. Let me explain why.

People always misunderstand having a humble mindset as opposed to having a go-getter mindset. The difference between you and a successful person is the difference in mindset.

When you think that you are not feeling well today to go to the gym. That you are not motivated enough to do some cardio or run that treadmill. That you didn't have a good day and now you are feeling down so you should stay in bed because you think you deserve some time off. This is the moment you messed up your life.

What you should have done is to tell yourself, What have I achieved today that made me deserving of this time off. You didn't!

How can you sit back and remain depressed when no one else feels sorry for you but only you do. Because you still haven't come to realize that no one will give you sympathy for something you made a mess of. And you are still not willing enough to make things happen for yourself.

When you have nothing, you think someone owes you something. That someone handles something bad that happens in your life. The reality is far from this.

It is fine if you are going through some rough patch in your life right now. But don't try to put the blame on others and back off of your responsibilities and duties. You have something to move towards but you are still sitting there waiting for the moment to come to your doorstep. But it ain't gonna happen. It's never an option to wait!

Don't just sit there and make strategies and set goals. Get up and start acting on those plans. The next plan will come by default.

You shouldn't feel depressed about the bad things, you should feel anger for why did you let those things happen to you in the first place. What did you lag that made you come to this stage right now. Why were you so lazy enough to let those results slide by you when your gut told you to do something different. But you didn't. And now it has all come to haunt you once again.

But you don't need that attitude. What you need is to stop analyzing and start doing something different rather than contemplate what you could have done.

The moments you lost will never come back, so there is no point in feeling sorry for those moments in this present moment. Use this moment to get the momentum you need.

Now is the time to prove yourself wrong, to make this life worth living for.

Now is the time to spend the most valuable asset of your life on something you want the most in your life. Now is the time to use all that energy and bring a change to your life that you will cherish for the rest of your life and in that afterlife.

Prove to yourself that you are worthy of that better life. That no one else deserves more than you. Because you made a cause for yourself. You ran all your life and struggled for that greater good.

Destiny carves its path when your show destiny what you have to offer.

You want to succeed in life, let me tell you the simplest way to that success; get up, go outside and get to work.

When you feel the lowest in your life, remember, you only start to lose that fat, when you start to sweat and you feel the heat and the pain coming through.

What you started yesterday, finish it today. Not tomorrow, not tonight, but right now!

Get working! It doesn't matter if it takes you an hour or 12 to complete the job. Do it. You will never fulfill the task if you keep thinking for the right moment. Every moment is the right moment.

You are always one decision away from a completely different life. You are always one moment away from the best moment of your life. But it is either this moment or it's never.

Chapter 5:

<u>Be Inspired to Create</u>

Some of you will look in the mirror today and think that you are weird. You will see that you are different to other people. That you are quirky or odd. But I want to encourage you. Not only is your uniqueness something that you should embrace but it is perhaps your greatest asset. The wonderful thing about people being different is that they think a little differently, see the world from a slightly different perspective. The combination of the various bits of knowledge that they have fit together in different ways.

When you speak you are most likely not conscious of your accent. Maybe if you live in a foreign country you are hyper aware of it. But how many of you know that your mind has an accent too. It has an accent that is formed from your experiences. Your experiences with pain. Your experiences with joy. Your experiences with success, failure and even your experiences with the everyday mundane. Not only that but the accent of your mind constantly evolves.

Why does that matter?

Because it is that accent which enables you to innovate. When you speak a foreign word, it takes on a new form in your accent – sometimes it may even be a sound that has never been uttered with that tone and inflection. It is completely original not because of the form of the word but because of the accent that informs the way the word comes out.

The same is true of your mind. You can speak the same ideas, study the same fields, even research the exact same thing and still end up with different outcomes. How? Because your outcomes are being informed by your experiences. Your ideas are your present thoughts running rampant through familiar thought patterns. They are tailored towards a particular style. For some of you it is like your mind rolls the r's in your ideas. It adds a certain *je ne sais quoi* to your ideas. To others your accent is thick and mutes the aesthetic nuances of ideas – manifesting in wonders of logic and mechanics.

Whatever it may be, I encourage you to embrace the accent of your mind. Actually, I demand you to. It is time that you stopped denying the world of your contribution to it. It's time that you got inspired to create. It is time that you allowed ideas to implode within the realm of your consciousness and innovations to pour out of it. Whether you find your language in art, dance, engineering, or politics. If you have a niche area of knowledge or see a pattern from a unique combination of information then it is about time you harnessed that and rode the creation train to wherever it may take you. I can promise you that you will never look back. We tend to regret the things we did not do, not the things that we did.

Listen closely and hear the accentuation of your thoughts. Then speak their creative ingenuity into being.

Create something that only you can.

Chapter 6:

Why You Are Setting The Wrong Goals

Ever wondered why you are not getting any closer to your goals? Why you keep failing despite having all that effort? Why does someone else seem to be more successful?

Here are some thoughts for you to ponder.

You may have a good set of skills and all the eligibility criteria anyone else has. But you are not yet in the same spot you wished some years ago. Maybe it is not happening for your right now, because your approach to those goals is not correct. Or, maybe your goals are wrong altogether.

Let's say you had a goal to be someone or achieve something someday. But you never had any idea how to! So you started asking why am I not getting the success that I deserve, but never asked yourself, how can I get to that success.

So you might think that you have the right goals to achieve something. But the reality is, that you never had the right goals.

You should have set a single goal a single day. A single goal that you can achieve in a day will help you get on the right train at the right time with a limited effort.

You shouldn't think of the future itself, but the goal that you might achieve someday. Once you have that goal in mind, you shouldn't need a constant reminder every day just to create a scenario of depression and restlessness that won't help you rather strain unnecessary energy.

Once you have the final goal, put it aside and work towards the small goals that you can achieve in real-time with actual small efforts.

Once you have a grasp of these goals, you will find the next goal yourself; a goal that you might have never thought of before.

Just say you want to lose weight and you want to get to your ideal BMI someday. This is a valid and reasonable Goal to achieve. This might prolong your life and increase your self-worth. So you should have a set of regular goals that ultimately lead you to the final goal.

So you want to lose weight, start by reducing fats and carbs in your next meal, and the one after that and the next one.

It will be hard the first time. Maybe the same at the second time. But when you have envisioned the ultimate goal, you will be content with the healthier alternates as well.

Add 5 minutes of exercise the next day, along with the goals of the previous day. You will be reluctant to do it the first time, but when you see the sweat dripping from your chin, you will see your healthier self in each drop.

Every goal has its process. No matter how much you avoid the process, you will always find yourself at the mercy of mother nature, and nature has always a plan for execution.

Now it's your decision whether to be a part of that process or go down in history with a blank face with no name.

You will always find a way to cheat, but to cheat is another ten steps away from your penultimate goal.

Make it your goal to resist every temptation that makes your day no different than the previous one. Live your life on One day, Monday, Change day principle and you will always find yourself closer to your salvation.

The process of change is mundane. In fact, the process of everything in life is mundane. You have to apply certain steps and procedures for even doing the most basic tasks in your daily life.

Stop procrastinating because you are not fooling anyone else, just yourself. And if you keep fooling yourself, you will be the worst failure in the books of history.

Chapter 7:

Doing The Thing You Love Most

Today we are going to talk about following your heart and just going for your passion, even if it ends up being a hobby project.

Many of us have passions that we want to pursue. Whether it be a sport, a fitness goal, a career goal, or simply just doing something we know we are good at. Something that electrifies our soul. Something that really doesn't require much persuasion for us to just go do it on a whim.

Many of us dare not pursue this passion because people have told us time and time again that it will not lead to anywhere. Or maybe it is that voice inside your head that is telling you you should just stick to the practical things in life. Whatever the reasons may be, that itch always seem to pester us, calling out to us, even though we have tried our best to put it aside.

We know what our talents are, and the longer we don't put it out there in the world, the longer we keep it bottled up inside of us, the longer the we will regret it. Personally, Music has always been something that has been calling out to me since i was 15. I've always dabbled in and out of it, but never took it seriously. I found myself 14 years later, wondering how much i could've achieved in the music space if i had just leaned in to it just a little.

I decided that I had just about put it off for long enough and decided to pursue music part time. I just knew deep down inside me that if i did not at least try, that i was going to regret it at some point again in the future. It is true that passions come and go. We may jump from passion to passion over the course of our lives, and that is okay. But if that thing has been there calling out to you for years or even decades, maybe you should pay closer attention to it just a little more.

Make your passion a project. Make it a hobby. Pursue it in one form or another. We may never be able to make full careers out of our passions, but we can at least incorporate it into our daily lives like a habit. You may find ourselves happier and more fulfilled should you tap that creative space in you that has always been there.

Sure life still takes precedence. Feeding the family, earning that income, taking care of that child. But never for one second think that you should sacrifice doing what truly makes you happy for all of that other stuff, no matter how important. Even as a hobby, pursuing it maybe 30mins a day, or even just an hour a week. It is a start and it is definitely better than nothing.

At the end of the day passions are there to feed our soul. To provide it will some zest and life to our otherwise mundane lives. The next time you hear that voice again, lean in to it. Don't put it off any longer.

Chapter 8:

Fight Is The Reward

There are times in our lives when we feel blocked out. When we feel the darkness coming in. When we see the sun going down and seemingly never coming back up. When the winds feel tougher and everything coming in your way puts you down like a storm.

No matter how big and how defiant you get, life will always find a new way to knock you down.

You will often find yourself in a place where you have nowhere to go, but straight. And that straight path isn't always the easiest too. It has all these ridges and peaks or a long ditch. So you finally come to realize that the only way out is a challenge itself and you can't bow out because there is no other way around.

I want you to understand the concept of fight and struggle. The success stories and breakthroughs we all hear are mostly just 2 parts; its 90% work and 10% fight.

We all work and we all work hard. But the defining moment of our journey is the final fight we go through.

The work we put in gets us to the bottom of the final barrier but the effort we need to summit the peak is the fight we put in and finally get the breakthrough. But fighting isn't easy. It is the hardest part of your journey to success.

The fight you need to put in isn't just the Xs and O's. The true fight is your mental toughness. It's your sheer will to keep going and keep pushing because you are just around the corner for the ultimate success.

You are just on the verge of finding the best reward of your life. You are on the cusp of seeing and enjoying your happiest moments. Because you have finally found your dreams and you have finally fulfilled your purpose in life.

Now is the time to rise and give up the feeling of giving up. Now is the time to get on top of your challenges. Now is the time to sweat and get over that pain.

This is the moment you need to be at your best. This is the time you need your A-game. This is the time to defy all odds and go all in. Because the finals moments need the final straw of strength and effort in your body.

Make a decision and become your own light. Believe in yourself like you have never before and you will never look back.

So if you ask me again why is fighting worth it. It's because your attitude makes you win long before you have even set the foot in the battleground. It's your will to keep going that makes you stand out even before getting into the spotlight.

You don't win a fight when you fight, you win a fight before the fight even begins. Your ultimate reward is the collection of all your efforts and resilience.

Chapter 9:

Hitting Rock Bottom

Today we're going to talk about a topic that I hope none of you will have to experience at any point in your lives. It can be a devastating and painful experience and I don't wish it on my worst enemy, but if this happens to be you, I hope that in today's video I can help you get out of the depths and into the light again.

First of all, I'm not going to waste any more time but just tell you that hitting rock bottom could be your blessing in disguise. You see when we hit rock bottom, the only reason that we know we are there is because we have become aware and have admitted to ourselves that there is no way lower that we can go. That we know deep in our hearts that things just cannot get any worse than this. And that revelation can be enlightening. Enlightening in the sense that by simple law of physics, the worse that can happen moving forward is either you move sideways, or up. When you have nothing more left to lose, you can be free to try and do everything in your power to get back up again.

For a lot of us who have led pretty comfortable lives, sometimes it feels like we are living in a bubble. We end up drifting through life on the comforts of our merits that we fail to stop learning and growing as people. We become so jaded about everything that life becomes bland.

We stop trying to be better, we stop trying to care, and we that in itself could be poison. It is like a frog getting boiled gradually, we don't notice it until it is too late and we are cooked. We are in fact slowly dying and fading into irrelevance.

But when you are at rock bottom, you become painfully aware of everything. Painfully aware of maybe your failed relationships, the things you did and maybe the people you hurt that have led you to this point. You become aware that you need to change yourself first, that everything starts with growing and learning again from scratch, like a baby learning how to walk again. And that could be a very rewarding time in your life when you become virtually fearless to try and do anything in your power to get back on your feet again.

Of course all this has to come from you. That you have to make the decision that things will never stay the same again. That you will learn from your mistakes and do the right things. When you've hit rock bottom, you can slowly begin the climb one step at a time.

Start by defining the first and most important thing that you cannot live without in life. If family means the most to you, reach out to them. Find comfort and shelter in them and see if they are able to provide you with any sort of assistance while you work on your life again. I always believe that if family is the most important thing, and that people you call family will be there with you till the very end. If family is not available to you, make it a priority to start growing a family. Family doesn't mean you have to have blood relations. Family is whoever you can rely on in your darkest times. Family is people who will accept you and love you for who you are inspite of your shortcomings. Family is people that will help nurture and get you back on your own two feet again. If you don't have family, go get one.

If hitting rock bottom to you means that you feel lost in life, in your career and finance, that you maybe lost your businesses and are dealing with the aftermath, maybe your first priority is to simply find a simple part time job that can occupy your time and keep you sustained while you figure out what to do next. Sometimes all we need is a little break to clear our heads and to start afresh again. Nothing ever stays the same. Things will get better. But don't fall into the trap of ruminating on your losses as it can be very destructive on your mental health. The past has already happened and you cannot take it back. Take stock of the reasons and don't make the same mistakes again in your career and you will be absolutely fine.

If you feel like you've hit rock bottom because of a failed marriage or relationship, whether it be something you did or your partner did, I know this can be incredibly painful and it feels like you've spent all your time with someone with nothing to show for it but wasted time and energy, but know that things like that happen and that it is perfectly normal. Humans are flawed and we all make mistakes. So yes it is okay to morn over the loss of the relationship and feel like you can't sink any lower, but don't lose faith as you will find someone again.

If hitting rock bottom is the result of you being ostracised by people around you for not being a good person, where you maybe have lost all the relationships in your life because of something you did, I'm sure you know the first step to do is to accept that you need to change. Don't look to someone else to blame but look inwards instead. Find time where you can go away on your way to reflect on what went wrong. Start going through the things that people were unhappy with you about and start looking for ways to improve yourself. If you need help, I am here for you. If not, maybe you might want to seek some professional help as well to dig a little deeper and to help guide you along a better path.

Hitting rock bottom is not a fun thing, and I don't want to claim that I know every nuance and feeling of what it means to get there, but I did feel like that once when my business failed on me and I made the decision that I could only go up from here. I started to pour all my time and energy into proving to myself that I will succeed no matter what and that I will not sit idly by and feel sorry for myself. It was a quite a journey but I came out of it stronger than before and realized that I was more resourceful than I originally thought.

So I challenge each and everyone of you who feels like you've hit the bottom to not be afraid of taking action once again. To be fearless and just take that next right step forward no matter what. And I hope to see you on the top of the mountain in time to come.

Chapter 10:

<u>10 Habits of Tiger Woods</u>

Eldrick Tont Woods, professionally known as Tiger Woods, was born on 30th December 1975 in Cypress, California in the United States. He was the only child of an African American army officer father and a Thai mother.

Here are ten habits of the golf legend, Tiger Woods:

1. <u>He is a fast learner.</u>

Eldrick was nicknamed Tiger by his father, Earl, in honor of a fellow soldier he served together with. He was his mentor and teacher and taught him how to play golf since he was very young.

The boy Tiger was a fast learner and he had become conversant with the game at the age of 8 years.

2. <u>He is hardworking.</u>

Tiger Woods is a very hardworking man since his childhood. He was able to balance both sports and academics, and he secured a place at Stanford University. At the University, he won several amateur U.S. golf titles.

He turned to professional sporting in 1996 and won the U.S. Masters the following year when he was only 22 years. His hard work and devotion crowned him the youngest person and first African American to win the tournament.

3. He is strong-hearted.

Woods had a strong connection with his father and the news of his death in 2006 came as a shocker to the sports giant. Tiger's mentor succumbed to prostate cancer and his son eulogized him profoundly.

Tiger was strong enough to manage the pain of his loss and returned to sports where he won the PGA Championship and the British Open.

4. He loves his family.

Tiger treasures family time so much that he took some time off to welcome his first child with his wife on 18th June 2007. His time off was ground for good family time for the first-time parents.

He also took another break from work when they had their second child, Charlie Axel Woods on 8th February 2009. His hiatus lasted for two weeks then he returned to play championship.

5. He is a fighter.

Tiger has had several accidents over his sporting career. He has had to severally undergo knee reconstructive surgery and return to the field. He has also suffered back injuries and had his fourth back surgery in 2017.

He at one time sought professional help to manage medication intake for pain and a sleep disorder. He seeks to survive all the medical complications that he undergoes and nothing has shut down his love for sports.

6. He is remorseful.

Tiger Woods has faced infidelity questions. He was rumored to be having an affair with Rachel Uchitel but he maintained a loud silence. Reports of other mistresses Tiger had emerged and on 2nd December 2009, he publicly apologized over unspecified mistakes.

As infidelity reports against Tiger increased, he once more apologized to his fans about his infidelity and owned up to his mistake. Tiger also apologized to his family, friends, and fans after he was arrested and charged for driving under the influence in May 2017.

7. He prefers quietness to talking things over.

The golf legend is a man of few words especially when he is on the wrong side. He uses silence as his weapon leaving the public to speculate the truth.

Even after photographic evidence surfaced of his affair with Rachel Uchitel and Tiger's wife reportedly broke the back window of Wood's SUV, Tiger Woods kept quiet and instead opted to drop out of his charity golf tournament.

8. He loves public relationships.

Tiger is a man who does not shy from keeping his relationships in the public. After his divorce from his wife, he confirmed to the media that he was dating Lindsey Vonn.

He also kept his relationship with his wife public and always announced major family events. After some time, Woods announced his breakup with Vonn because their busy schedules kept them apart.

9. He is honest.

Tiger Woods is largely an honest man. He once lied about his mistresses before divorcing his wife. He however led a very honest life thereafter. In October 2017, he pleaded guilty to reckless driving and agreed to enter a program for first-time offenders. It was unexpected but Tiger chose to learn his lesson the hard way.

10. He knows how to nurse himself back to health after surgery.

Tiger Woods is among the few sportspeople who have undergone many surgeries because of their sport. He has emerged victorious after every medical procedure he has had to go through.

After resuming playing golf from medical-related complications, Tiger has managed to secure a good position in the rankings.

In conclusion, these are ten habits of the golf legend – Tiger Woods. The 46-year-old golfer has created a name for himself in the history of the sport.

Chapter 11:

<u>10 Habits of Jeff Bezos</u>

As you know, your lifestyle choices can make or break your success. It began in a basement and has since grown into a well-known online shopping app. Jeff Bezos' brainchild, the "Everything Store," is a platform where people get online deals. Commonly known as Amazon.com, the "Everything Store" is billion dollars' worth.

Jeff Bezos' habits vary from what to read to dealing with stress, which he phrases as "laugh a lot." Bezos, the self-made millionaire and Amazon CEO, is one of the world's wealthiest persons. But, what got him there? His natural aptitude for business got him there. Moreover, his habits are key to his achievements.

Here are ten business-oriented Jeff Bezos' habits for innovative-minds upkeep.

1. Customer-Centric Approach

Unlike most of the business, Bezos and Amazon have in decades ignored a "profitable" approach to doing business; instead, he invests in a customer-centric approach. Although at some point Amazon got chastised by publishers for allowing the laity to evaluate books, Amazon encouraged its consumers to share their comments, whether critical or negative.

An incentive that created a Clientele review platform which is why Amazon.com is today's most trusted e-commerce platform. Keeping a soundtrack of your customers means that you're taking good care of them.

2. Make Your Plan Based on Things That Will Not Change

While trading your brands-be it, lipstick, tractor seats, e-book readers, or data storages, make bigger plans with these constants: Provider your clientele with a broader selection scope, lower pricing, and rapid, dependable delivery.

3. Create Your Own Rules

If you despise writing essays, Amazon might not be the place for you. Amazon made it a rule early that anyone who wishes to suggest a new concept must first condense their views into a six-page booklet.

Before making any decisions, everyone concerned, must read and analyze the six-pager. And also, according to Bezos, "no team should be so large that two pizzas won't be enough." When your organization is far larger to be fed by two pizzas, divide it into fewer independent units of your own liking and capabilities to compete for limited resources while making your customers happy.

4. Work Backwards to What Your Customers Require

Customers' desires, rather than drivers' preferences, have shaped the specifications for Amazon's significant new projects, such as the Kindle tablets and e-book readers. So if your clientele doesn't want something, let it go, even if it means dismantling a once-powerful department.

5. Master the Art of Failure

Bezos's Amazon recruited many editors to produce book and music evaluations but later decided to use user feedback instead. A move that failed miserably.

Such blunders, according to Bezos, are a normal part of your innovative life, as long as you're on a learning reality, failure is sometimes positive. To succeed as an innovator, means that you are in for such flaws as taking risks, failing at a point while tucking your sleeves for a changes.

6. Make Informed Choices or Decisions

If you did know that Amazon began as a bookstore, well, here you have it! Bezos' product decisions are always a product of well thought logics and factual data rather than incidental incentives. Your product decision should be knowledgeable, and reading is knowledge.

In a nutshell, books are the ideal driver for e-commerce. Because nearly every aspect of commerce and customer behavior can be quantified, and almost all choices are based on data. Meetings are about metrics, not tales from customers!

7. You Are Willing To Be Misinterpreted for a Long Time

Many of Bezos-Amazon's initiatives appear as money-losing distractions. Which severally send the company's stock price down and earns the wrath of focal analysts. A five-to-seven-year financial plan is acceptable if your new initiatives make strategic sense to you.

8. Don't Mind the Competition

If your business is imitating and engrossed in what others are doing, then you're off Jeff Bezos' innovative strategies. In truth, client service should always come first. Just as Amazon Prime, succeed in your innovative plans while satisfying your clientele-base.

9. Don't Try To Be a Blockbuster

Your present success does not guarantee your future relevance. Consider the fate of Blockbuster Video and accept the fact that your industry advances with time, and will never hold similar standing as of now. Pay close attention to evolving state of affairs as you lead the change rather than reacting to it.

10. Ditch Complexity

Startups are characterized by rapid decision-making and innovation. However, as a company grows, it is frequently delayed by complexity. This suffocates innovation. Just like Bezos, always treat your company as a start-up at the cutting edge.

Conclusion

Following Jeff Bezos uniqueness will not guarantee you $100 billion. But you'll still set yourself up for a more prosperous future with your company endeavors if you maintain this proactive, forward-thinking approach.

Chapter 12:

Why You're Demotivated By Lack of Clarity

Clarity is key to achieving any lasting happiness or success.

Demotivation is almost certain without clarity.

Always have a clear vision of what you want and why you want it.

Every detail should be crystal clear as if it were real.

Because it is.

Mustn't reality first be built on a solid foundation of imagination.

Your skills in visualisation and imagination must be strong to build that foundation.

You must build it in the mind and focus on it daily.

You must believe in it with all your heart and your head will follow.

Create it in the mind and let your body build it in reality.

That is the process of creation.

You cannot create anything in reality without clarity in the mind.

Even to make a cup of coffee, you must first imagine making a cup of coffee.

It doesn't take as much clarity as creating an international company,

but focus and clarity are required nonetheless.

The big goals often take years of consistent focus, clarity and commitment.

That is why so few succeed.

Demotivation is a symptom of lack of direction.

To have direction you must have clarity.

To have clarity you must have a clearly defined vision of you future.

Once you have this vision, never accept anything less.

Clarity and vision will begin your journey,

but your arrival depends on stubbornness and persistence.

Before you start you must decide to never quit, no matter what happens.

Clarity of your why will decide this for you.

Is the pain you are about to endure stronger than your reasons?

If you are currently demoralised by lack of clarity,

sit down and decide what will really make you happy.

Once you have decided, begin to make it feel real with pictures around your house.

Listen to motivational music and speeches daily to build your belief in you.

Visit where you dream you will be one day.

Get a feel for your desired new life.

Create actions that will build clarity in your vision.

Let it help you adjust to your new and future reality.

Slowly adjust your vision upwards.

Never adjust downwards.

Never settle for less.

The more real your vision feels the more likely it will be.

Begin to visualise living it.

Before long you will be living it.

Adopt the mannerisms of someone who would be in that position.

When you begin to believe you are important, others will follow.

Carry yourself like a champion.

Soon you will be one.

Have clarity you have about who you are.

Have clarity about what you are going to do.

Motivate yourself to success.

Once you step on that path you will not want to return to the you of yesterday.

You will be committed to becoming even better tomorrow.

You will be committed to being the new person you've always known you could be.

Always strive to get another step closer to your vision.

Work until that vision becomes clearer each day.

Have faith that each week more opportunities for progression will present themselves to you.

Clarity is the key to your success.

Chapter 13:

Bounce Back From Failure

Failure is a big word. It is a negative word most say. It is cursed in most cases. It is frowned upon when it is on your plate. But why?

Sure, it certainly doesn't feel good when you encounter failure. We can't even forgive ourselves for failing at a simple card game. We get impatient, we get hopeless and ultimately we get depressed on even the smallest of failure we go through in everyday life.

Why is it that way? Why can't we try to change a failure into something better? Why can't we just leave that failure right there and not try to make a big deal out of each and every small little setback?

These questions have a very deep meaning and a very important place in everyone's life.

Let's start with the simplest step to make it easy for yourself to deal with a certain failure. Whenever you fail at anything, just pause for a second and talk to yourself.

Rewind what you just went through. Talk to yourself through the present circumstances. Think about what you could have done to improve at what you just did. Think about what you could have done to prevent whatever tragic incident you went through. Or what you could have done to do better at what you felt like failing at.

These questions will immediately sketch a scenario in front of your eyes. A scenario where you can actually see yourself flourishing and doing your best against all odds.

Whatever happened to you, I am sure you didn't deserve it. But so what if you

Lost some money or a loved one or your pet? Ask yourself this, is it the end of the world? Have you stopped breathing? Have you no reason left to keep living?

You had, you have, and you will always have a new thing, a new person a new place to start with. Life has endless possibilities for you to find. But you just have to bounce back from whatever setback you think you cannot get out of.

Take for example the biggest tech billionaires in the world. I am giving this example because people tend to relate more to these examples these days. Elon Musk started his carrier with a small office with his brother and they both lived in the same office for a whole year. They couldn't even afford a small place for themselves to rent.

There was a time when Elon had to decide to split his last set of investments between two companies. If he had invested in one, the other would have gone down for sure, just to give a chance to the other company to maybe become their one big hit. Guess what, he ended up keeping them both because he invested in both.

Why did he succeed? Was it because he wasn't afraid? No!

He succeeded because he had Faith after all the failures he had faced. He knew that if he kept trying against all odds and even the obvious risks, he will ultimately succeed at something for what he worked so hard for all this time!

Chapter 14:

How to Deal with Stress Head On?
7 Things You Can Start Today

Drop your shoulders, release your tongue from your palate. Unclench your teeth and let your brows relax. You see, this is how stressed you are all the time, you forget completely about how it is affecting your body.

In this roaring river of the 21st century, we are all feeling the tide rising and falling 24/7. It will be a white lie if any of you claim to never feel stressed. We are all under varying degrees of stress all the time.

So what is stress exactly? Stress is not merely a stimulus or a physical response of our bodies but a process by which we appraise and cope with environmental threats and challenges. When expressed in short bursts or taken as a challenge, stressors may have positive effects. However, if stress is threatening or prolonged, it can be harmful for us.

So how then do we handle it?

It seems like quite a drag for most of us and pretty annoying a lot of the time, but here are several ways we can deal with it and come out of it stronger than before.

7 Tips to Deal with stress and anxiety

Number 1: Go To Bed Early and Wake up Early

Have you heard the quote "Early to Bed, early to rise, makes a man healthy, wealthy and wise."? When was the last time you went to sleep early? I believe that going to bed early is something we all know we need to do but hardly ever do.

Starting your day off early has many wonderful biological effects. Mornings tend to be cool, silent, serene, and distraction-free. This calmness helps bring our stress levels down and prepares us for the day ahead. By practicing some deep breathing techniques in the morning, it will also aid in flow and circulation throughout our bodies, something that is good for the mind and soul.

Number 2: Start Practicing Yoga or meditation

Yoga and meditation, while they are two separate practices, they overlap in many key areas. Yoga poses are great for us to engage with our bodies, to stretch out our muscles, tight sections of our bodies, and to help us focus on our breath at all times. Each yoga pose targets a unique meridian of our bodies, many allowing us to release tensions that might otherwise have built up without realizing. You can try simple poses such as a child pose or shavasana, or downward dog, to get yourself started.

Meditation on the other hand focuses stilling the mind through focus on the breath as well. Letting our thoughts flow freely, we are able to acknowledge the stressors we face without judgement. Try out some guided mindfulness meditation practices to get your started.

Number 3: Having Proper Time Management

Many of us overlook the importance of proper time management. We often let our crazy schedules overwhelm us. By being unorganized with our time, we are also unorganized with our emotions. If we let our calendar be filled with chaos, there is no doubt that we will feel like chaos as well. Stress levels will be bound to rise. Have proper blocks of time dedicated to each task in your day. Trust me you will feel a whole lot more in control of everything.

Number 4: Make time for your hobbies

We should all strive to live a happy and balanced life. If work is the only thing on our agenda, we will have no outlet to destress, relax, recharge, and be ready to face new challenges that might tax our physical and mental abilities.

Whatever your hobbies are: baking, tennis, crafting, surfboarding, or even shopping, as long as you plan them in your schedule and do them, you will definitely feel a whole lot better about everything. Let out all the steam, stress, anxieties, as you engage in your hobbies, or even just forget about them for a minute. Give yourself the space to breathe and just enjoy doing the fun things in life. Life isn't just all about work. Play is equally important too.

Number 5: Music is food for your soul

Music has many therapeutic qualities. If you feel your stress levels rising, consider popping your earbuds into your ears and playing your favorite songs on spotify. If you are looking for calm, you may want to consider listening to some chill music as well.

The kind of your music you listen to will have a direct effect on your mood and the way you feel. So choose your playlists wisely. Don't go heavy metal or goth, unless of course it helps calm you down.

Number 6: Start Cleaning your clutter

This may seem like I am quoting a movie where the stressed teenage girl decides to clean her room when she is feeling low. I'd say movies are made out of someone's real experience.

Cleaning your room or clutter can be one of the best therapies.

A messy space is a recipe for anxiety and stress. When we see clutter, we feel cluttered. Once you clear all the stuff you don't need, you will feel much lighter instantly.

Number 7: Allow nature to heal you

Nature is amusing and wonderful. Everything in nature is closer to our basic making than anything that we are dealing with today. So try getting close to nature, it will make you feel relaxed and at the same time enable you to enrich your brain.

Watch the sun setting into the sky and wake up to look at the colors at dawn.
There is nothing more beautiful in this world that we get to experience every single day no matter where we are on this earth.

Take a stroll in your favourite park, go for a cycle, a jog, or even just a stroll with your pet. Allow nature to melt away your stress and bring your peace.

Final Thoughts

Stressors are a part of life. Something we cannot escape from. But if we put in place some healthy habits and practices, we can reduce and release those negativities from our bodies, cleansing us to take on more stress in the future.

Chapter 15:

Being Mentally Strong

Have you ever wondered why your performance in practice versus an actual test is like night and day? Or how you are able to perform so well in a mock situation but just crumble when it comes game time?

It all boils down to our mental strength.

The greatest players in sports all have one thing in common, incredibly strong beliefs in themselves that they can win no matter how difficult the circumstance. Where rivals that have the same playing ability may challenge them, they will always prevail because they know their self-worth and they never once doubt that they will lose even when facing immense external or internal pressure.

Most of us are used to facing pressure from external sources. Whether it be from people around us, online haters, or whoever they may be, that can take a toll on our ability to perform. But the greatest threat is not from those areas... it is from within. The voices in our head telling us that we are not going to win this match, that we are not going to well in this performance, that we should just give up because we are already losing by that much.

It is only when we can crush these voices that we can truly outperform our wildest abilities. Mental strength is something that we can all acquire. We just have to find a way to block out all the negativity and replace them with voices that are encouraging. to believe in ourselves that we can and will overcome any situation that life throws at us.

The next time you notice that doubts start creeping in, you need to snap yourself out of it as quickly as you can, 5 4 3 2 1. Focus on the next point, focus on the next game, focus on the next speech. Don't give yourself the time to think about what went wrong the last time. You are only as good as your present performance, not your past.

I believe that you will achieve wonderful things in life you are able to crush those negative thoughts and enhance your mental strength.

Chapter 16:

How To Use Affirmations For Success

Affirmations are best described as a self-help strategy that is used to promote self-confidence and belief in your abilities. There might come a million instances where you felt like you needed to affirm yourself, and there would be many moments when you have probably affirmed yourself without even realizing it. Simple sentences like "I've got what it takes" or "I believe in my ability to succeed" shift your focus away from the perceived inadequacies or failures and direct your focus towards your strengths. While affirmations may not be a magic bullet for instant success, they generally work as a tool for shifting your mindset and achieving your goals.

Neuroplasticity, or our brain's ability to adapt and change to different circumstances throughout our lives, makes us understand what makes affirmations work and how to make them more effective. Creating a mental image beforehand of doing something that you're scared of, like acing a nerve-wracking interview or bungee jumping to conquer your fear of heights, can encourage your brain to take these positive affirmations as fact, and soon your actions will tend to follow.

Repeating affirmations can help you boost your confidence and motivation, but you still must take some action yourself. Affirmations are a step towards the change, not the change itself. They can also help you to achieve your goals by strengthening your confidence by reminding you that you're in control of your success and what you can do right now to achieve it. Affirmations give you a list of long-standing patterns and beliefs, and it makes you act as if you've already succeeded. Understand that affirmations alone can't produce a change in every situation. You have to take some actions too along with them. Similarly, affirming your traits can also help you see yourself in a new light.

To get the most benefits from affirmations, start a regular practice and make it a habit. Say affirmations upon waking up and getting into bed; give them at least 3-5 minutes. Repeat each of your affirmations ten times, focus on the words that leave your mouth. Believe them to be true while saying them. Make it a consistent habit. You have to be patient and stick with your practice, and it might take some time before you see evident changes. Practicing affirmations can also activate the reward system in your brain, which can impact how you experience both emotional and physical pain. The moment you start managing your stress and other life difficulties, it would help you promote faith in yourself and boost self-empowerment.

Chapter 17:

5 Ways Quitting Something Can Bring You Joy

Do you ever wonder if you will ever be truly happy in your life? Do you wonder if happiness is just a hoax and success is an illusion? Do you feel like they don't exist? I know a friend who felt like this a little while ago. At the time, she was making a six-figure income, was working for her dream company (Apple), and had a flexible work schedule. Despite all this, she was miserable. She would have never been able to quit my job if not for the practice she got from quitting little things.

Of all the things that she tried, quitting these seven little things made her the happiest.

1. Quit Reading the News

News headlines are usually about happenings around the world. Most times, they are negative. Negative headlines make for better stories than positive headlines. Would you read a headline that says 'Electric Chair Makes a Comeback' or a headline that says 'Legislation debate in Tennessee'? See what I mean.

Journalists have to write stories that interest us. I can't blame them for that. Changing the time that I caught up on the news helped me be more positive during the day. Start reading inspirational posts first thing in the morning instead of news. You can still catch the news later, around 11 am instead of at 6 am.

2. Quit Hunching Your Shoulders

This boosted my confidence levels.

We hunch our shoulders and take up as little space as possible when we feel nervous and not too comfortable. This is body language 101.

Keeping a posture, opening up your shoulders will make you feel more confident during the day. But, I must admit it will make you more tired than usual. It will take you at least a total of 45 days before you start doing this effortlessly.

3. Quit Keeping a Corporate Face at Work

We are all trained not to show real feelings at work. Having a corporate face is good for corporate, not for you. Smiling all day, even when you are upset, will lift your mood. It will make you feel better sooner. Studies have shown that smiling makes you happy.

4. Quit Writing Huge Goals

It is better to write and work towards achievable goals before starting to write our stretch goals. Stretch goals are great to push ourselves. But, we all need achievable goals to boost confidence and to have successes that we can build momentum on. This can be hard for you if you are an overachiever.

5. Quit Eating Fries and Eat Oranges Instead

Fries are comfort food for a lot of people. But eating them saps energy.

Eat oranges instead of fries every time you feel down and feel the need for comfort food. This not only boosts your energy but will also help you lose some pounds if you want to. Plus, this will give you energy and clarity of mind.

Chapter 18:

Stop Lying To Yourself

What do you think you are doing with your life? What do you keep on telling everyone you are up to? What ambitions do you make for yourself? What ideas do you follow? What goals do you want to follow and do you really have no choice in any of these?

These are not some random rude questions one might ask you. Because you deserve all of them if you still don't have anything meaningful in your life to stand behind.

You need to find a real achievement in your life that can make you feel accomplished.

Life is always a hard race to finish line with all of us running for the same goal of glory and success. But not all of us have the thing that will get us to that line first. SO when we fail to get there, we make reasons for our failure.

The reality is that it is never OK to make excuses for your failure when you weren't even eligible to join others to start with.

You have been lying to yourself this whole time, telling yourself that you have everything that takes to beat everyone to that finish line!

You have been lying to yourself saying that you are better than anyone there who came well prepared!

You keep telling yourself that you have a better understanding of things that you have just seen in your life for the first time! That you have a better approach towards life. That you know the best way to solve any problem.

Well, guess what my friend, You are wrong!

You don't have it all in you, you never did and you would probably never will. Because no man can master even one craft, let alone every. You need to do your homework for everything in your life, you try to master everything you come across but you can never really do so because you are a human. It is humanly impossible to be perfect at everything.

So stop calling yourself a saint or a self-taught genius because you are not.

You have this habit of lying to yourself because you find an escape from your faults. You find a way to cope with your inabilities. You find a way to soothe yourself that you are not wrong, just because everyone else says so.

You have to understand the fact that life has a way to be lived, and it is never the way of denial. It is rather the hopeful and quiet way of living your life with hard work and freedom.

You have to make your life worth living for. Because you know it in the back of your head that you have done the necessary hard work before to be able to compete among the best of the best out there.

You must have a strong feeling of justice towards yourself and towards others that makes you feel deserving of the highest honors and the biggest riches. Because you worked your whole life to be able to stand here and be a nominee for what life has to offer the best

Chapter 19:

<u>10 Habits For A Clean Home</u>

A clean home can make the homeowner a lot happier, less stressed, and even calmer. Waking up or coming back to a clutter-free and organized home can instantly brighten our mornings or even lift up our moods. But the thought of having to clean it extensively on weekends, for long hours, only to find the space in an absolute mess by midweek is like a nightmare and crestfallen.

Trust me when I say it is not that difficult maintaining a clean home. You need not necessarily have to deep clean your house almost every weekend for hours if you incorporate few very habits in your everyday routines. Today, we are exactly going to talk on this topic and hope to enlighten you to create a clean space.

Here are ten habits for a clean and happy home:

1. Make Your Bed As Soon as You Wake Up

We have heard a million times that the first thing that we should do after waking up is to make our beds, but how many of us incorporate this habit daily? An unmade bed can pull down the overall appearance of your bedroom by making it look messy. So take few moments and tuck those sheets and put your pillows in order. Change your bed sheets or duvet covers, and pillow covers as and when necessary.

Making our beds clean our most comfortable and visible area in the house and gives a sense of achievement helps us stay motivated and in a fresh state of mind throughout the day. If tucking in bed sheets daily is too annoying for you simply switch to duvet covers; that might save you from some hassle.

2. Put Things Back in Place After Using Them

Almost every home has this one chair or one spot that is cluttered with clothes and random knick-knacks, and this area hardly gets cleaned. Moreover, it is a normal human tendency to go on to dump more and more pieces of stuff and increase the pile size.

The idea behind creating this pile is that you will put away all the things in one go in a single day, but who are we kidding? As the pile starts increasing, we start pushing away the task of keeping the things back in their original place. The best way to avoid creating clutter is to put things back in their true place as soon as their job is done.

I completely understand that after finishing a task, we never feel like getting up to put them back in their home and hinder the task until we feel like doing so. But if you can consciously put this little effort into not letting things sit on the ground or in random places and put them back as soon as their job is done for the day, it is going to save a lot of time and help you have a clean space.

This is also applicable to your freshly washed clothes. As soon as you have them cleaned, fold them and put them in the drawer where it belongs. This will save you the headache of doing so on a Saturday morning which can then be used for reading your favorite book.

3. Take Your Mess With You as You Leave the Room

This is another essential practice that can bring a huge difference in your life and your home if turned into a habit. The idea here is to try not to leave a room empty-handed. What does this mean?
Let us take an example to understand this. Suppose you are in your living room and are going to the kitchen to drink water. Before you leave the living room, scan the room and look if any dirty bowl or plate is sitting in the room that needs to go to the kitchen. Take that cutlery along with you and keep them in the sink or dishwasher.

After making this a habit, you can then start following the one-touch rule that states that you touch a used item only once! That means if you are taking out the trash, make sure to dump or dispose of it properly and not just take it out and keep it somewhere on the porch or garden as this will kill the whole idea behind the habit. If you are moving something, it is better that you keep them where they belong, else, leave them be.

4. Have a House Cleaning Schedule

Maintain cleaning schedules like morning cleaning routines or weekly cleaning routines. This is basically distributing the cleaning of the entire house over an entire week rather than keeping the task to get done in a single day. Fix days for achieving a particular task, like on Wednesdays you can vacuum the living room and the bedroom and on Thursdays clean the other rooms and so on.

Make sure to assign 15 to 20 minutes each morning that you will strictly use for cleaning purposes. This will surely bring about a very positive impact on your house, and you will be in awe of how much cleaning can be done in those mere 15 - 20 minutes. Try to vacuum the hallways, entries, and all other high traffic regions of your home (including the kitchen) as frequently as possible as they tend to get dusty easily.

5. Maintain a Laundry Routine

Maintain a proper laundry routine depending on whether you live alone or in a family. As the pile of clothes grows enough to go into the washing, do the needful immediately. Do not delay the task endlessly as remember it is always easier to wash one load of clothing at a day rather than washing multiple loads of cloth in a day.

If you live with a family, do laundry every alternate day and if you live alone, then make sure to do your laundry every weekend. Also, make it a habit of putting the dirty clothes in the basket immediately after changing out of it rather than keeping them at random places to wash them later.

6. Keep Your Shoes, Coats, and Umbrellas in Their Right Place

Make it a habit to open your shoes near the entrance, put them away properly, and not randomly throw them. Keep a basket near the entryway where you can store all the umbrellas. If possible, put up a key holder on the door to keep the car keys and door keys in an organized manner.

The same goes for your long coats. Do not just dump them anywhere right after returning home! Have hooks hidden behind the entry door or have a sleek cupboard near the exit to store the trenchcoats and the long coats away from sight. These little changes will instantly clean up space.

7. Relax Only After Finishing Your Chores

If you have a chore that requires immediate attention, do it! Do not sit and relax, as this will go on to delay the chore indefinitely, and you may even forget to do it. So get your chores done first, then sit and watch Netflix. Detain your tasks only when you are exhausted and desperately need a break.

8. Clean After Every Meal

Right after fishing your meal, clean up the place. I know what most of you are thinking, but trust me, relaxing after cleaning everything up will give you more satisfaction and help you have a cleaner home for sure. After having your lunch or dinner, keep all the plates in the washer and make sure to also clean the utensils that you used for cooking.

Clean the countertops, the burners, and also the table that you sat and ate on. Cleaning the countertops and tables immediately will save your furniture from an ugly stain and help you save a lot of energy and time you might have had to put in if you try to clean the spill the later day.

9. Clean Your Dishes and Sink Every Night

I wanted to say have a nighttime cleaning routine every day where you clean all the dishes from dinner or any other remaining dishes of the day, the sink, and the kitchen by placing all the ingredient containers in their rightful places. The nighttime routine would also include setting your dining table, setting the cushions on your sofa, and clearing out your fridge so that you have a clean and spacious fridge before you unpack your groceries.

But I understand that not many of us have the energy after a hectic day at work, so instead of doing the entire routine, just make sure to wash all the dishes and clean the sink thoroughly so that you wake up to a beautiful kitchen in the morning. I mean, who wants to wake up to a pile of dishes, right? Just give some extra time at night to clean out the kitchen to have a fresh start in the morning.

10. Get Rid Of Unnecessary Things

To have a clutter-free space, each item in your home must have a home of its own. For example, if you do not have a place to hang your towels, they will likely be lying here and there and making the space look messy. Thus, make sure each item has its own place to sleep. If you see there are free-flowing items, then it is time to declutter!

You do not need much space, but you definitely need fewer items that fit in the available space and are easier to manage. More items require more time to clean and put things away properly. Thus, it is easier and requires less time to clean a room with lesser items out on the floor or on the countertop. Hence, make it a habit of getting rid of all the unnecessary items. You can donate the items or gift them to your neighbors or friends. Recycle all the old newspaper and magazines as papers too contribute a lot to the messiness of any room.

Extra Tip: Always try to keep your cleaning supplies in easily visible and accessible areas. This will save you a lot of time and motivate you to clean up anything that should be done as soon as possible.

Be satisfied with clean enough! A home can neither be squeaky clean every day nor can it be cleaned in one day. It is a gradual process that requires a conscious effort being made daily.

A clean home can be easily achieved by following these tips and manifesting these practices as your daily habits.

Chapter 20:

<u>10 Habits That Give Me Joy</u>

Joy is an innate feeling of extreme happiness that one experiences. It bubbles within your spirit before it manifests physically for others to see. Unlike happiness, joy is not easily put off because it is brought by your actions without external influence. Do acts that will satisfy you and impact the people around you positively.

These are ten habits that will bring you joy:

1. <u>Belief in God</u>

Human beings feel the need to believe in a superior being. Almost everyone believes in the existence of a superior deity that sustains life. He is God. The relationship between God and man is like that of a parent and their children. Their presence in the lives of their children is very important because they provide for their needs and protect them from the harsh world.

When you believe in God, you will not have to worry about issues beyond your control because God will take care of you. He will guide you through life and lead you away from worldly sorrows. Your joy will be akin to that of a child who walks beside their parents. They have nothing to worry about.

2. Staying Debt-Free

Shackles of debt have tied people and nations to their debtors. They always look over their shoulders to see if someone is after them especially when it is time to service their debt. This denies you the joy of life in living as a free person.

Avoid entering into unnecessary debt regardless of how flexible the terms of service could be. Debt is attractive because it promises to solve your problems instantly. However, it only postpones the reality to some future date. You will have joy when you live your life within your means and not enter into debt to sustain your needs.

3. Living My Ideal Dream

Quite a handful of people live their ideal lives. While growing up we have a fantasy of the kind of life we would want to live, the nature of families we would want to have, and the type of work we want to do. Sometimes miss part of our dream package but still, life has to move on.

You live your ideal life when you fulfill any of your dreams in life because not everyone gets such a blessing. People are stuck in jobs they dread but cannot quit because they have to fend for themselves and their families. It is joyous to live life as you had envisaged.

4. Success In My Work

Our work and businesses are sources of income in our lives. They pay our bills and sustain our needs. Life is rough when business is not favorable. We would do everything possible to maintain our jobs or business because we rely on them.

We are joyous whenever we get promoted at work, or when our businesses flourish. Our mastery of skills could seal our opportunities. Whatever your specialty could be, perfect your skills at work and you will be successful. Success at work will bring you joy in life.

5. A Well-Knit Relationship With Family and Friends

We are social beings and are interdependent. No man is an island. At any point in our lives, we need the support of other people no matter how much we try to dissociate ourselves.

When you have a healthy relationship with your family and friends, you will unconsciously attract joy. How beautiful it is to have a shoulder to lean on during hard times! They will comfort and encourage you when your spirit is low. Cultivate a healthy relationship with them and you will live a joyful life.

6. Mentoring Someone

People will forget what you said but will never forget how you made them feel. Be careful how you present yourself to people and guard your reputation at all costs. You never know who could be watching.

There is joy when you mentor someone to walk into your steps and watch them grow. You can associate yourself with their success and achievements. It is a form of investment in a person that can never go bad. Your impact can be felt even in your absence. It is as if you are reincarnated.

7. Exploring The World

The world has diverse cultures and there is always something new to learn. Do not be tied to your locality because your thinking will be limited to only what you can see. Familiarity breeds contempt. When you stay at one place for long, people will get tired of you and take you for granted. They will overlook your presence and you will be depressed about it.

Traveling to new places brings the joy of a child because of new experiences. You will be happy to discover new things and exchange ideas with other people. The reason why children are always joyful is that they always find small things fascinating, unlike adults who are familiar with everything in their environment.

8. Adapting To Change

We cannot escape from change no matter how hard we try. It is impossible to live as you did a few years ago and ignore how much the world has changed. Those who live in denial are depressed because of their inability to adapt to change.

You will attract joy if you are flexible in life. Nobody has a monopoly of ideas on how to live life. Do not be rigid in what you know because you will be disappointed when it is no longer fashionable.

9. Be Content And Appreciative

Staying content is a rare trait to find in a world where people's ambitions have clouded their judgment, making them irrational. You will always be bitter if are not appreciative of what you have because there is always somebody who is one step ahead of you in life.

Being content does not stop you from being ambitious. Joy comes when you derive satisfaction from the simple things in life. Do not wait for greater things for you to be joyful. Joy comes in small packages that we often overlook.

10. Develop Hobbies

Hobbies are what we do to relax from our busy schedules. They are what we do apart from work. We can do them alone or with the company of other people. It could be swimming, singing, traveling, playing soccer, reading novels, or writing.

Hobbies attract joy because there is no pressure to perform and nobody to judge us. You can be yourself with no one to please but yourself.

In conclusion, there is a distinction between joy and happiness. Joy comes from within you while happiness is greatly influenced by other people in our lives. These ten habits bring me joy, so shall they to you if you consider them.

Chapter 21:

If You Commit to Nothing, You'll Be Distracted By Everything

I don't think anyone in their right mind would like to face a challenge where they have a chance to face failure or even a possibility of it.

We all need a new lesson to learn. A lesson of commitment and conviction. A lesson of integrity, grit, and sheer will. One might ask, why should I adopt the features of a soldier rather than a normal social being. Why do I need to go to extremes?

The answer to these questions is simple yet heavy, with a load most people avoid their whole life.

We all have somewhat similar goals. We all want to be in a better place in better shape. We all want wealth. We all want healthy stable relationships. We all want respect and a million other things.

Ask yourself this; Have you ever actually tried hard enough for any of this to happen. Have you ever tried to dig deep till you found your last breath? But it felt good because you had a good enough reason and passion to pursue?

The goals of life are a compulsion to have. We all must have something to strive for. Something worth fighting for. Something we can look back and be happy about.

But having a goal and committing to it are two different things.

One can have a goal and still not be motivated enough to do anything in their power to achieve that thing. No matter how the road takes turns.

We need to have the inspiration to drive us through the rough patches of life. To make us keep pushing even if we get squeezed within the incidents happening around us.

Don't take this the wrong way but you have to accept the fact that whatever you are feeling has nothing to do with what you want to achieve. Because what you want to achieve is something that your life depends on. The goals you set aren't some wishes or a feeling that your gut gives you. These goals are the requirements of life with which you can finally say lived a happy successful life. And this statement is the ultimate purpose of your life.

You were given this life because you had the energy to go for things that weren't easy, but you had the potential to achieve these. All you needed was a little commitment and Zero distractions.

The commitment you need isn't a feeling that goes and on and off like a switch. Rather a distinct key for the lock of your life.

So if you still think you will have days where you can try one more time, Let me be clear; You better start thinking about the future of your next generation. Because I don't think they'd have one.

You need to be committed enough to do anything that takes you closer and closer to your goals and nothing that wastes a second out of your life.

Because either you go all in or you walk the line and hedge your bets. The bet here being your life.

Chapter 22:

<u>10 Habits of Roger Federer</u>

Roger Federer is a Swiss professional tennis player who has won 20 Grand Slams, sharing a record with Rafael Nadal and Novak Djokovic (The Big Three). Federer has been the world No. 1 in the ATP rankings for a total of 310 weeks, including a record 237 consecutive weeks, and has closed the year-end as No. 1 five times.

Roger Federer has achieved unprecedented success in his profession as well as in other areas of his life. He is lauded as the best tennis player of all time with his dominance play style that combines excellent footwork and shot-making abilities. He has been honoured with the Laureus World Sportsman of the Year award four times in a row. Giving a glimpse of his axioms for success, Federer shared a couple of his slogans.

Here are the ten habits of Roger Federer.

1. Hard Work

After the 2016 Wimbledon break due to knee injury, Federer come back claimed the Australian Open crown, defeating his arch-rival Rafael Nadal. His response to this excellent comeback was simple: "work the hardiest." The foundation of your career success is your consistent hard work.

2. Establish Strategic Goals

Roger Federer excels at setting both short and long-term objectives. He understands that short-term goals provide a cause for his daily habits to continue and that long-term ambitions include winning other Slams and legacy continuation. Maintain a laser-like concentration on your priorities and decline any offers that may jeopardize your long-term aspirations. Trust your long-term strategy, but keep your short-term goals intact for daily motivation.

3. Learn From the Chase

Roger Federer lives for the lessons he's learned throughout his journey. When he was young, he wanted to be the best tennis player in the world. That sparked a chase and a long journey to realize his boyhood desire. Pursue your passions with all your heart, but don't lose sight of the importance of your trip.

4. Rest Is an Important Productivity Metric

Federer usually schedules rest days following the Slams and other important tournaments. He also gets 11 to 12 hours of sleep per night. Rest is an essential aspect of Federer's career longevity. And like Federer, you may find yourself revived and ready for the next assignment after some well-deserved downtime.

5. To Evolve, Adapt

Between 2012 and 2017, Federer was overshadowed by Novak Djokovic, to whom he lost three finals. However, retiring was not near his thoughts but despite his age, he set out to become faster, stronger, and with an intensified killer instinct. As you get older, you become more concerned with quality than quantity because quantity harms the body.

6. Question Yourself Always

Success journey is complex; hence you must be willing to be your harshest critic. Federer has achieved a great deal of success because he is constantly questioning himself. His success bar is so high that he seeks out any flaw he can find and carves it out until it becomes a strength. Don't be too kind to yourself!

7. Learn New Skills

Identify the abilities you need to excel at your profession and continue enhancing those skills. For nearly two decades, Federer and his fitness coach, Pierre Paganini, worked hard from a young age to develop his fastness, a crucial quality in tennis. Well-deserved reward will come if you put in appropriate action.

8. Build on your strengths

Working on your shortcomings, according to Federer makes you a better player but does not make you dangerous. His extra focus goes on building on shots that his opponents find it hard to exploit can't exploit.

9. Maintains Cool in Stressful Situations

Roger, by now, is your role model for being calm in challenging and pressurized situations. When he was younger, he was highly emotional, frequently complaining and hurling rackets. He was wasting a lot of energy, which was preventing him from functioning well. He worked hard to improve his mental game, and he is now one of the finest mental performers in the sport.

10. Serve Others

Through the Roger Federer Foundation(RFF), Roger has been aiming to make a difference in the world by creating quality lives for underprivileged children, particularly in Africa. Just like Federer, use your platform to make the world a better place.

Conclusion

Federer is a model athlete. He dedicated almost his entire life to tennis, kept his head down, and worked diligently for decades to become the greatest player of all time. When you're good at anything, make it your primary focus.

Chapter 23:

<u>10 Habits of Larry Page</u>

These days, children learn to google before they stroll, and a considerable part of the credit goes to Larry Page, the largest and most popular search engine one of the biggest innovators of our time. Larry Page, alongside his co-founder Sergey Brin, founded what has grown into one of the world's largest empires: the Google-search engine.

Nobody can simply ignore it: everybody else enjoys Google -apart from libraries. Page, could later step as CEO of Google to manage Alphabet, a technology company making waves across several industries. His success and conviction in what became the world's search engine set him apart from the start.

Here are ten worth mentioning Larry page's success habits for your success path lessons.

1. Pay Attention to Your Gut

If you're great in what you do, always respect your gut. Decisions are frequently made in haste due to time constraints, and if you have a gut sense that your choice is correct, you should go with that gut feeling. You may succeed or fail, but trusting yourself is pivotal for your well-being.

2. A Clear Vision

One key factor in Larry Page's success is knowing where he wanted to go, knowing where you want to go getting there much more accessible. Define your purpose in a single sentence to ensure that you truly understand what you want to achieve; if you can't, your goal isn't clear enough.

3. Focus on Your Strengths

When it comes to getting your things done quickly, you need to know where your strengths are. However, in some instances, you'll need to work on your weaknesses. This way, be sure of generating your finest work ever.

4. You Wouldn't need A Big Company to Make Your Idea a Reality

Google, Amazon, Apple, and Disney have in common is that all began in a garage with few resources but big dreams. So you only need to gamble on it, believe in your idea and go forward with determination to achieve your goals even if you lack the essential means at the time.

5. Allow Your Dreams To Direct Your Actions

All of your activities will become a lot easier to take after you've discovered your calling. All is required is your effort put in realizing your goals.

When you know what you genuinely want in life, the way to get there becomes a little clearer. Of course, there will always be ups and downs, but it is simpler to know what you are going for.

6. Don't Delegate, Do It Yourself

Most go-getters struggle with delegating work to others when they don't have the time to devote to them. Many leaders learn to let go, but Page was resistant to this change in his natural management approach early in his career. Make every effort to hasten the process. Though the verdict on the efficiency of this managerial approach is still out, it worked in Page's favour. Instead of wasting your efforts delegating, continue doing what you are incredibly great at.

7. You're Working on Changing the World

According to Larry's page, you're doing the right thing if your thing is benefiting the people. For your business to work well, the problems are solved, and demands met. Find a loophole in your society; let it count if you'll be part of the solution.

8. Learning Is Continuous

Larry Page once remarked, "the main things in life are to live, learn, and love." So follow your curiosity and take risks in your endeavours. Don't give up on your ambitions.

Nothing brings you more joy than reaching your goals and realizing your dreams; believe in your dreams because they may be able to sustain you for the long haul.

9. You Are Trust-Worth-People Have Trust in You

It would help if you won the trust of others, in this case, your audience-before they would believe in you. So focus on your audience's demands, maintain a presence on social networks where your target audience is, and carry out various actions to gain the trust of your potential clients, such as providing quality material or providing excellent customer service.

10. You are Respectful

People are your company's most valuable asset, and you should never lose sight of this. If you treat your staff with the same respect that you do your clients and potential clients, you will notice that they will treat your firm with the same regard.

Conclusion

In 2012, while still Google's Ceo, Larry Page told his investors, "whatever you can imagine is possible. Comfort is the worst friend a successful business can have, therefore avoid it at all costs and try to put some effort into every work you perform and every goal you seek. As your everyday work is exciting, could you keep it going? No holding back!

Chapter 24:

Your Motivational Partner In Life

We all have friends. We all have parents. We may have a partner or other half. We all have teachers.

We love and respect all of them and hopefully, they do too. But have we ever wondered why we do that?

Why do we have to love someone who brought us into this world? Why do we love a person who is not related to us whatsoever, but has a connection with us, and hence we like to hang around them? Why do we respect someone who is being paid to do what makes him respectable?

The answer to all these is simple. They make us a better version of ourselves. Without these people in our lives, we won't be as good as we are right now.

It doesn't matter where we stand right now in our lives, there would always be someone backing you up whenever you feel low.

People tend to seek loneliness and a quiet corner whenever life hits hard. But what they don't realize is that there are people in their lives who have a duty towards you.

Either that be your parents or friends or partner or anyone for that case, you need to find time to give them a chance to show their true affections towards you. You need to give them

Your parents can't give up on you because you are a part of them. You have their legacy to keep and spread. They want you to be a better person than they ever were, hence they will always support you no matter what the world does to you.

Your friends have a bond of loyalty towards you which is the basic root of any friendship. They will always try to help you get up no matter how many times you fall.

All these people owe you this support. And you owe it to them to be a source of inspiration when they want a shoulder to cry. When they want a person to listen and feel their pain. When they need someone to be able to share some time with them without a grain of self-interest.

These things make us stronger as a human and make us grow and evolve as a Specie.

You can find motivation and inspiration from anyone. It may even be a guard in your office or a worker in your office who you might see once a week.

Basic human nature makes us susceptible to the need of finding company. It doesn't matter where it comes from. What you need is a person who can devote a selfless minute of his or her life to you and feels good when they realize they have made a positive change in your life.

Everyone goes through this phase of loneliness but we always find a person who makes us the most comfortable.

The person who reimburses our self-belief. The person who makes us take one more try, one more chance, not for us but for them too. This person is your true motivational partner in life.

Chapter 25:

10 Ways To Build New Habits by Taking Advantage of Old Ones

You may have heard that old habits die hard or that a leopard never changes its spots. It is easier to build new habits on old ones than to form them from scratch.

These are ten ways to build new habits by taking advantage of old ones:'

1. Replacing Strategy

This is a psychological strategy of deceiving the mind that you are following your old habits while it is not the case. It works best if you had an addiction that you want to get rid of. For example, alcoholics who want to reform can replace beer with soft drinks or even coffee and take it at the same time they use to take a beer.

The new habit will gradually overshadow the old one and after some time it will be completely gone.

2. Change Your Company

Take an audit of your friends and their habits and you will observe that you share some things, including the habit you want to get rid of. You cannot overcome it if you are constantly in their company because of the influence they have over you.

Take a step of distancing yourself from them and watch yourself adapting to the new habits you desire. In their absence, you will find other friends with whom you will share the new lifestyle of your choice.

3. Engage In Sports and Recreational Activities

So powerful is sports that it unites warring sides and rival communities. Spend the time you used to do a habit you want to abandon to engage in any kind of sports. It is a good replacement for that time and it exposes you to other people who may influence you to other new positive habits. Moreover, you will be exhausted after the games and will not have the time to return to your old habit.

4. Invest Your Time in Researching On Demerits of Your Old Habits

Divert your energy, time, and resources to researching the harm they cause instead of engaging in them. You will be enlightened and with the knowledge build a new habit of creating awareness about the same to save other people.

You will effectively create a new habit to replace the undesirable older one.

5. Use The Old Habit As A Motivation For A New One

When life gives you lemons, make lemonade. Leverage the positive aspect of every situation including your old habits to create new ones. The motivation to abandon your old ways will help you build new habits that are the opposite of the old ones.

This is effective especially if you want to build a reputable reputation.

6. Combine Two Habits

You can combine two habits to help build a new one if you want to retain all of them. You can clean the house while singing and dancing to your favorite song. You will ride on the singing and dancing to fortify your cleaning skills.
This method will make you an all-around person and likable.

7. Express An Old Habit In A New Way

New habits are not always new. They can be a recreation of old habits. Change how you approach issues to give birth to a new habit.
If you love storytelling, for example, consider doing the same through blogs or videos. In the process, you will adopt a writing habit.

8. Seek Professional Guidance

If you are comfortable sharing your experiences with somebody else, talk to a professional counselor or a trustworthy person. They will be your light and advice you on the path to pursue when you are in limbo.
When we have fully discovered ourselves, we can build new habits on old ones. At times, we need the guidance of experienced people and professionals to discover our hidden abilities.

9. Change of Environment

Our environments play a significant role in unearthing our potential. Different environments have different challenges to which we adjust differently. Sometimes a change in our environments is important to help us develop new habits from our old ones.

We could be blind to how we can use our old habits to our advantage when we are in one place for a long time.

10. Seek Financial Freedom

Building new habits from old ones could sometimes require some funding. For example, you may want to go to the movies but you are unable to finance that. When you are financially stable, you can easily adjust yourself in situations that require financial muscles.

In conclusion, these ten habits are not the only ones to help build new habits by leveraging on old ones. They are however the most effective ones.

Chapter 26:

10 Habits of Michael Phelps

With 28 medals, 23 of which are gold, Michael Phelps is the greatest and most decorated Olympian in history. His career included five Olympic Games and two decades of supremacy. Even though Phelps competes in a sport where exceptionally talented athletes can win gold medals over various distances and strokes, his achievements dwarf those of any other athletes.

His competitive nature and a strong desire to always win have everything to do with his breakthrough. How did Phelps become the world's most excellent swimmer?

Here are the ten habits of Michael Phelps.

1. Dream Big and Set Outlandish Goals

According to Phelps, "the more you dream, and your goals, the more you achieve greatness." He desired a swimming career and had goals of becoming the best. He had to put in a lot of effort to attain his ambitions, including earning a gold medal at the Olympic Games. You won't achieve anything unless you dream big and set lofty aspirations.

2. Dare Doing New Things

Nothing is impossible, according to Phelps, as long as you are willing to try it out. Phelps understands how tough it is to win an Olympic gold medal, but he was motivated to do it and make history. Don't step back from trying new things because you are not sure of the outcomes.

3. Believe That Anything Is Possible

Phelps was able to become the finest swimmer in the world because he believed in himself. He also believes that God answers prayers of those who have faith and strive hard to achieve their goals. You must believe that anything is possible as you strive to achieve it.

4. Utilize Both Your Strengths and Weaknesses

Michael Phelps is well-known for his athleticism. His workouts are tough, and has best genetic attributes. However, he has ADHD and uses it as fuel for his swimming. Just like Phelps, your strengths and weaknesses are your biggest motivation.

5. Maintain Strict Self-Control

There is no quick way to greatness. You must put in the effort if you want to be successful at anything. For Phelps to be a world-class athlete, you must sustain world-class actions. He trains for 6 hours a day, seven days a week. When he is not doing physical training, he rests, allowing his muscles to relax while meditating and visualizing.

6. Don't Give Up

Michael Phelps is a real example of how you shouldn't allow your failures define or ruin you. Just triumph over them no matter what. Remember how Phelps' reputation was tarnished after he was detained from his drunk and drinking habits? Despite the anguish, he always came back strong.

7. Get a Puppy

Phelps has a dog named Herman, a bulldog he adores and makes him more responsible. Moreover, it helps him in managing his ADHD. Having a pet makes you more accountable, empathic, compassionate, and disciplined.

8. Give It Your Best

Phelps physical traits-his hands and feet can function as paddles, and his height form glides effortlessly through the water. For sure, he was a swimmer! Michael learned of his exceptional talent and persisted in becoming an Olympic champion. It would be great if you always practiced what you are best at to excel in it.

9. Survive the Odds for Success

When his career was setting off, Phelps achieved zero notable positions. He lost in several championships, which crushed him as a young swimmer. He did not, however, quit. He trained harder than ever before, and in the 2008 Beijing Olympics, he won eight gold medals, breaking the record for the most gold medals won in a single sport. Hung in there, despite the setbacks, persevere, and eventually, you'll triumph.

10. Be Self-Assured Enough To Declare Your Aspirations

There was no doubt that Michael was born to be a legend, and he was not afraid to let the world know about it. His pride in letting people know his plans to win several gold medals was constantly chastised as arrogance, but his fans always had his back. Yes, there will be sceptics, but letting your friends and family in to a portion of your goals keep you motivated.

Conclusion

There is doubt that Michael Phelps is an excellent swimmer and a champion given that he has set and broken several world records. Just like Phelps, your career, personal life, and other areas of your life will be defined by your daily routine. His habits are definitely a 100% worth of mentoring you towards being the best you can be.

Chapter 27:

Stop Ignoring Your Health

Do you have a busy life? Do you follow a hard and continuous regime of tasks every day for a significant amount of time? Have you ever felt that you cannot enjoy even the happiest moments of your life even if you want to? Let me highlight one reason you might recognize it straight away.

You are not enjoying your days while still being in all your senses because you don't have your mind and body in the right place.

All these years you have lived your life as a race. You have taken part in every event in and around your life just because you never wanted to miss anything. But in this process, you never lived your life to its full potential. You never lived a single moment with just the emotional intention of being then and there and not trying to live it like just another day or event.

People often get so busy with making their careers that they don't realize what is more important in life? It is their mental and physical health!

You will not get anywhere far in your life if you keep ignoring the signs of sickness your body keeps giving you. Your body is a machine with a conditional warranty. The day you violate the conditions of this warranty, life will become challenging and you won't even be interested in the basic tasks at hand.

You might have heard the famous saying that "Health is Wealth". Let it sink in for a while and analyze your own life. You don't need to be a top-tier athlete to have a good body. You need a good body for your organs to work properly. You need an active lifestyle to be more productive and be more present and engaged in the things that are going around you.

The dilemma of our lives is that we don't care about what we have right now, but we care a lot about what we want. Not realizing that what we want might be cursed but what we have is the soul of good living. And that my friends are the blessing of health that most of us take for granted.

Most people have a tendency and devotion to work specifically on their health and fitness on a priority basis. They have a better standard of life. These people have a clearer mind to feel and capture the best moments in life with what their senses can offer best to them.

If you don't stop ignoring your health, you won't ever get out of this constant struggle. The struggle to find the reasons for you being detached from everything despite being involved every time.

Being careful and observant of your health doesn't make you selfish. This makes you a much more caring person because not only your life but the life of others around you is also affected by your sickness. Not only your resources are used for your treatments but the attention and emotions of your loved ones are also being spent, just in hope of your wellness.

Chapter 28:

Motivation With Good Feelings

Ever wonder what goes on in your mind when you feel depressed isn't always the reaction to the things that happen to you? What you go through when you feel down is the chemistry of your brain that you yourself allow being created in the first place.

You don't feel weak just because your heart feels so heavy. You feel weak because you have filled your heart with all these feelings that don't let you do something useful.

Feelings are not your enemy till you choose the wrong ones. In fact, Feelings and emotions can be the strongest weapon to have in your arsenal.

People say, "You are a man, so act like one. Men don't cry, they act strong and brave"

You must make yourself strong enough to overcome any feelings of failure or fear. Any thought that makes you go aloof and dims that light of creativity and confidence. It's OK to feel sad and cry for some time, but it's not OK to feel weak for even a second.

Your consciousness dictates your feelings. Your senses help you to process a moment and in turn help you translate them into feelings that go both ways. This process has been going on from the day you were born and will continue till your last day.

You enter your consciousness as soon as you open your eyes to greet the day. It is at this moment when your creativity is at its peak. What you need now is just a set of useful thoughts and emotions that steer your whole day into a worthwhile one.

Don't spend your day regretting and repressing things you did or someone else did to you. You don't need these feelings right now. Because you successfully passed those tests of life and are alive still to be grateful for what you have right now.

There are a billion things in life to be thankful for and a billion more to be sad for. But you cannot live a happy fulfilling life if you focus on the later ones.

Life is too short to be sad and to be weak. When you start your day, don't worry about what needs to be done. But think about who you need to be to get those things done.

Don't let actions and outcomes drive you. Be the sailor of yourself to decide what outcomes you want.

Believe me, the feeling of gratitude is the biggest motivator. Self gratitude should be the level of appraisal to expect. Nothing should matter after your own opinions about yourself.

If you let other people's opinions affect your feelings, you are the weakest person out there. And failure is your destination.

Visualization of a better life can help you feel and hope better. It would help you to grow stronger and faster but remember; The day you lose control of your emotions, feelings, and your temper, your imagination will only lead you to a downward spiral.

Chapter 29:

How to Value Being Alone

Some people are naturally happy alone. But for others, being solo is a challenge. If you fall into the latter group, there are ways to become more comfortable with being alone (yes, even if you're a hardcore extrovert).

Regardless of how you feel about being alone, building a good relationship with yourself is a worthy investment. After all, you *do* spend quite a bit of time with yourself, so you might as well learn to enjoy it.

Being alone isn't the same as being lonely.

Before getting into the different ways to find happiness in being alone, it's important to untangle these two concepts: being alone and being lonely. While there's some overlap between them, they're completely different concepts. Maybe you're a person who basks in solitude. You're not antisocial, friendless, or loveless. You're just quite content with alone time. You look forward to it. That's simply being alone, not being lonely.

On the other hand, maybe you're surrounded by family and friends but not relating beyond a surface level, which has you feeling empty and disconnected. Or maybe being alone just leaves you sad and longing for company. That's loneliness.

Short-term tips to get you started

These tips are aimed at helping you get the ball rolling. They might not transform your life overnight, but they can help you get more comfortable with being alone.

Some of them may be exactly what you needed to hear. Others may not make sense to you. Use them as stepping-stones. Add to them and shape them along the way to suit your lifestyle and personality.

1. Avoid comparing yourself to others.

This is easier said than done, but try to avoid comparing your social life to anyone else's. It's not the number of friends you have or the frequency of your social outings that matters. It's what works for you.

Remember, you have no way of knowing if someone with many friends and a stuffed social calendar is happy.

2. Take a step back from social media.

Social media isn't inherently bad or problematic, but if scrolling through your feeds makes you feel left out and stresses, take a few steps back. That feed doesn't tell the whole story. Not by a long shot.

You have no idea if those people are truly happy or just giving the impression that they are. Either way, it's no reflection on you. So, take a deep breath and put it in perspective.

Perform a test run and ban yourself from social media for 48 hours. If that makes a difference, try giving yourself a daily limit of 10 to 15 minutes and stick to it.

Don't be afraid to ask for help.

Sometimes, all the self-care, exercise, and gratitude lists in the world aren't enough to shake feelings of sadness or loneliness.

Consider reaching out to a therapist if:

- You're overly stressed and finding it difficult to cope.

- You have symptoms of anxiety.

- You have symptoms of depression.

You don't have to wait for a crisis point to get into therapy. Simply wanting to get better and spending time alone is a perfectly good reason to make an appointment.

Chapter 30:

<u>10 Habits of Novak Djokovic</u>

The just-concluded French Open may probably have thrilled you, whether you are a tennis fan or not. With Novak Djokovic breaking more records and giving away his racket as a souvenir to a young boy. The Siberian Tennis Player is now ranked No. 1 in the world in men's singles. Djokovic's recent win isn't something new; he has been ranked no. 1 by ATP for over 300 weeks throughout his entire career. In 2016, he became the first player to hold all four Grand Slams simultaneously since Rod Laver, becoming one of the best players ever. Mesmerized by his tennis skills?

Here are 10 Novak Djokovic habits.

1. Envision Huge Dreams

According to Novak Djokovic says, embracing the process towards the world's best may belong, and tough, but it will pay you off. He used to watch Pete Sampras play and win, and it's when he started envisioning his win and made himself a trophy to that. When you believe in the possibility of achieving something, it becomes easier to learn skills for doing it.

2. Discipline and Dedication

Success is a consequence of many years of hard work and dedication. Your daily habits matter in everything. At only seven years, Novak had a burning desire to become the finest tennis player the world could ever have. Which later gave him the precision of what he needed to do. He devised a strategy for how much practice he would need to put in to become the best throughout his career.

3. Keep Improving

Limitations are merely mental constructs. Constant winning and growth require that you keep on enhancing your current skills. Because if you stop, others will catch up and surpass you. Novak is not the same as years ago; his desire to always top has led him to explore new things that potentially improve his game.

4. Master the Serve Return

Return serve proficiency is a vital shot in tennis. Novak is an excellent server; he has won more points on first and second return serves. Achieving such proficiency requires that you first make a body turn before moving your arm. This gives your body control and precision when returning the first serves. Moreover, you're able to take a bigger swing at the ball when your opponent's second serve seems average or weak.

5. Mental Struggles Is Part of the Sport

It can be so damaging to your confidence when you lose after dominating the tennis world for years. However, no one is immune. You have seen it with Tigger Woods in golf, and indeed, Novak has had his own to cope with. Pressure is part of tennis and a challenge to players. Accept and learn how to live with it.

6. Flexibility Is All It Takes

Flexibility is one of those aspects that, while vital in principle, is frequently overlooked in practice. For Tennis players, it is more on injury prevention than performance. Moreover, if you must maximize performance while preventing injury, how flexible you are saying it all. Novak has demonstrated flexibility as a weapon for maintaining balance and stability when tackling the game from extended positions.

7. Perseverance Is Key to Competitiveness

The route to the top is a rocky ride of ups and downs and mysterious impediments. It took Novak a journey of many continuous losses to reclaim his throne-which is a doubled challenge having been a dominant tennis player, but that's tennis. Tennis is very competitive, and the sooner you realize this, the better.

8. Better Late Than Never

Djokovic rose to prominence much later than his famous opponents, Federer and Nadal. When he won his first Grand Slam, they had already won many Grand Slams-though now he is at par with them. It also took time to be included in the list of the "big three." All you need is to act, work hard, and enjoy the game.

9. Don't Focus on Popularity

Surprisingly, and for a long time, Djokovic had no huge audience like his rivals, which could be noticed when he was up against them. Instead of letting this get to him, he turned it into motivation and fought extra hard. Let your accomplishments only raise your fan base.

10. Diet

Know your health issues, and stick to the diet your body needs. During the 2010 season, Novak experienced fatigue during matches. He lacked stamina and struggled with respiratory difficulties. He found out, with the help of a dietitian, that he was gluten and dairy intolerant.

Conclusion

Like Novak, whatever comes in your professional life is a product of discipline, dedication, and inspiration that comes from within you.

Chapter 31:

8 Habits That Make People Dislike You

As human beings, we all have a deep innate need to be liked. It's very easy for someone to make a sweeping judgement based on their first impression of you. The vast majority believe that being likable is a matter of natural, inexplicable traits that only belong to a fortunate few; good looks, fierce social media, among others. The reality is that every detail matters; from your interpersonal skills, your last name, your smell, and so on. Generally speaking, certain behaviors make people hold back from liking you. Unless you get such habits done with, it's always easy to fall prey to the unlikeable discrepancy.

Here are 8 habits that makes people dislike you.

1. Self-Indulgence

On the top of the list is a self-centered person. If you are always talking about yourself, greedy, or simply just so full of it, it's not easy to understand why people will find you very annoying. If you are always bragging about your triumphs or lamenting about your problems, be prepared for people to avoid you. If the talk is just about you, and you always, you will be avoided at all costs. Focus on others and their problems instead of your own. Let them share their thoughts and ideas with you equally; that is the basic foundation of a conversation. Don't be full of yourself!

2. **Being Too Serious.**

People are drawn to enthusiastic individuals. However, because they are often absorbed in their work, enthusiastic people can become too serious or uninterested. This is a turn off as people will find you likable only when you take pride in work while paving way for fun moments too. Which means that you are serious with whatever you are doing but also cherish those socially fun times. This, in turn, demonstrates that the moments you share with others are just as important as your work.

3. **Narrow-Mindedness and Rigidity.**

When you are open-minded, you are easily likable and approachable. This is in contrast to rigidity and narrow-minded traits. When you are conversing with someone, you must be willing to accept all opinions that differ from yours, even if you don't always agree with them. You may not like what everyone has to say all the time, but it does not imply that you start picking fights and arguing about every small matter. An open-minded person is approachable and so likable. People can talk to you about anything because they know you will not be upset. They will not fear being judged by you because you portray a neutral aura.

If you go into a debate with preconceived views, you are unable to see things from someone else's perspective. It will lead to disputes and arguments. Nobody loves someone who is rigid and judgmental.

4. **Dishonesty and Emotional Manipulation**

One of the most typical traits of unlikable people is dishonesty. Everyone lies at some point in their lives, but people begin to avoid you when lying becomes a habit. You may lose good friends as a result of this tendency. Dishonest people are frequently manipulative. Instead of confessing their shortcomings, they would tell a lie to avoid an awkward scenario. They can concoct a thousand lies to conceal a single fact. If you engage in the habit of lying, people will quickly see your true colors and you may see your friends dropping like flies.

5. **You Are a Gossip Mogul.**

When people get carried away with gossiping, they make themselves look awful. Wallowing in gossip about other people's actions or misfortunes may end up hurting their feelings if the gossip reaches them. What's more, it's that gossip will always make you look unpleasant and bitter. People will associate you with as the person who goes around spreading rumors and misinformation to others. You may begin to be viewed as untrustworthy in other people's eyes and people will stop telling you things.

6. **A Name-Dropper.**

One of the most vexing hobbies of unlikable people is name-dropping. It is advantageous if you know a few influential and well-known people. Name-dropping in every conversation, on the other hand, will make you obnoxious and unlikable. Name-dropping is a characteristic of insecure persons who are always looking for attention. People will know who you are with without you having to mention it on every occasion. Nobody likes someone who always feels the need to appear superior or more important than others. Sure it'll be interesting to engage in conversations about these people you know, but do it wisely.

7. **You Are Constant Phone-Checker.**

Checking the phone while having a moment with someone is one of the worst habits of dislikeable people. It is just awful! You should opt out of it.

When you are alone, it is ok to look at your smartphone. However, continuously checking your phone while eating dinner with someone or attending a meeting is impolite. It implies that you are not paying attention to the person who is trying to have this conversation with you. Being addicted or glued to your phone all the time will give the impression that nothing is more important to you than your screen time. You will find that it turns people off and you may not get asked out for a meal again. Don't be so distracted. Pay attention to the person all the time.

8. **Sharing Too Much Information, Too Soon.**

Chatting up with others necessitates a decent standard of sharing; sharing too much about yourself straight away however, may be inappropriate. Take caution not to share personal concerns or admissions too early.

Likable people allow the others to direct them when it is appropriate for them to open up. Oversharing might have an impression that you are self-centered and unconcerned about conversation balance. Consider this: if you dive into the details of your life without first learning about the other person, you're sending the impression that you consider them as nothing more than a sounding board for your troubles.

Conclusion

If you're still wondering why others dislike you, look again at the above signs and habits of unlikable people. Being likable has nothing to do with being gorgeous or intelligent! All you have to do is respect other people's time and opinions. When spending time with someone, you must pay close attention. Being open-minded, sensitive, and understanding automatically makes you likable. When you become more conscious of how other people perceive your behavior, you pave the route toward being more likable.

Chapter 32:

How To Set Smart Goals

Setting your goals can be a tough choice. It's all about putting your priorities in such a way that you know what comes first for you. It's imperative to be goal-oriented to set positive goals for your present and future. You should be aware of your criteria for setting your goals. Make sure your plan is attainable in a proper time frame to get a good set of goals to be achieved in your time. You would need hard work and a good mindset for setting goals. Few components can help a person reach their destination. Control what you choose because it will eternally impact your life.

To set a goal to your priority, you need to know what exactly you want. In other words, be specific. Be specific in what matters to you and your goal. Make sure that you know your fair share of details about your idea, and then start working on it once you have set your mind to it. Get a clear vision of what your goal is. Get a clear idea of your objective. It is essential to give a specification to your plan to set it according to your needs.

Make sure you measure your goals. As in, calculate the profit or loss. Measure the risks you are taking and the benefits you can gain from them. In simple words, you need to quantify your goals to know what order to set them into. It makes you visualize the amount of time it will take or the energy to reach the finish line. That way, you can calculate your goals and their details. You need to set your mind on the positive technical growth of your goal. That is an essential step to take to put yourself to the next goal as soon as possible.

If you get your hopes high from the start, it may be possible that you will meet with disappointment along the way. So, it would be best if you made sure that your goals are realistic and achievable. Make sure your goal is within reach. That is the reality check you need to force in your mind that is your goal even attainable? Just make sure it is, and everything will go as planned. It doesn't mean to set small goals. There is a difference between big goals and unrealistic goals. Make sure to limit your romantic goals, or else you will never be satisfied with your achievement.

Be very serious when setting your goals, especially if they are long-term goals. They can impact your life in one way or another. It depends on you how you take it. Make sure your goals are relevant. So, that you can gain real benefit from your goals. Have your fair share of profits from your hard work and make it count. Always remember why the goal matters to you. Once you get the fundamental idea of why you need this goal to be achieved, you can look onto a bigger picture in the frame. If it doesn't feel relevant, then there is no reason for you to continue working for. Leave it as it is if it doesn't give you what you applied for because it will only drain your energy and won't give you a satisfactory outcome.

Time is an essential thing to keep in focus when working toward your goals. You don't want to keep working on one thing for too long or too short. So, keep a deadline. Keep a limit on when to work on your goal. If it's worth it, give it your good timer, but if not, then don't even waste a second on it. They are just some factors to set your goals for a better future. These visionary goals will help you get through most of the achievements you want to get done with.

Chapter 33:

How To Crush Your Goals This Quarter

Some people find it very hard to achieve their goals, but luckily, there is a method waiting to be used. The quarter method divides the year into four parts of 90-days; for each part, you set some goals to crush. The rest of the year has gone, and so have the three quarters; now it is time to prepare for the fourth quarter. 1st October is one of the most critical days in the life of a person who sets his goals according to the quarter. It is the benchmark representing the close of the third quarter and the beginning of the fourth quarter. It is the day when you set new goals for the upcoming three months; if somehow your third-quarter dreams were not crushed, then you can stage a comeback so you wouldn't be left behind forever. But how to achieve your fourth-quarter goals?

1st October may bring the start of a quarter, but it also ends another quarter; it is the day when you focus on your results. Have you achieved the goals you set for the third quarter? If not, then prepare yourself to hear the hard truth. Your results reflect your self-esteem; if you believe in yourself, then you would achieve your goals. If you are not satisfied with your results, think, is this what you had in mind? If no, then having small visions can never lead to a more significant impact. Limiting beliefs will never give you more than minor and unimpressive results. Your results tell you about your passion for your work; if you are not passionate about your work, you would have poor outcomes. We all have heard the famous saying, " work in silence and let your success make the noise," but what does this mean? It means that your results will tell everyone about your hard work. If your results are not satisfactory, you know that the problem is your behavior towards your work.

When setting goals for the future, one needs to accept the facts; what went wrong that put you off the track? The year is 75% complete, and if you still haven't crushed your goals, you need to accept that it is your fault. If you blame these failures on your upbringing, your education, or any other factor than yourself, then you are simply fooling yourself because it is all dependent on you. When you don't achieve what you wanted to in nine months, you must have figured the problem; it can be any bad habit you are not willing to give up or the strategies you are implying. If you pretend your habits, attitude, and approach are just fine, you are just fooling yourself, not anyone else. This benchmark is the best time to change the old bad habits and try forming some new strategies.

To finish the year with solid results, you need to get serious; the days of dissatisfied results are gone, now it is time to shine some light on your soul and determine what you are doing wrong, what habits are working in your favor, and which ones are not. Then you can decide which habits to give up on, which habits to improve, and which ones to keep. Once you have sorted this out, prioritize your goals and set some challenging destinations to avoid getting bored or feeling uninterested. When setting deadlines, try to set enforceable deadlines.

Confusion can lead to poor results, so sit back and think about the goals that I should not pursue. This is called understanding goal competition; the goals you set are competing for your time. Actual peak performance comes from understanding which goals to pursue and which not to seek. And when you complete a plan, don't just rush into the process of crushing the next goal; allow yourself to celebrate your win and feel the happiness of the goal finally getting destroyed by you.

Chapter 34:

How Not To Waste Your 25,000 Mornings As An Adult.

Adulthood is the time of our lives when we need to get serious about everything. We have to take care of every single thing from time to our mornings. Early morning is the time of the day when freshness consumes us—known as the best time to work. Why waste such precious time? Having a good morning automatically means having a good day too. When a mind is fresh, it works. And wasting 25,000 mornings of your adulthood would be truly foolish. Those 3571 weeks would go to waste as there was no essential work done.

To make sure that you don't waste your morning is to be sure that you have mornings. Waking up late just automatically means that half of your day has gone to waste. So, wake up early. Those early hours have some courage to work in them. And who wants to waste such an opportunity to prove themselves. Not only will it be beneficial for your professional life, but it will also be beneficial for your health. Get a decent night's sleep, and you will see the changes that come along with them.

After you open your eyes in the morning, immediately sit up. Going back to sleep is always a more intriguing option. But we need to know that our priority is to wake up. And when you are sleeping, make sure that nothing disturbs it. Phone on silent—the tv's off and lights out. Make sure you are as comfortable as possible so you won't wake up the following day grumpy. Disturbance in sleep may cause the disappearance of it. There is a chance that you can't sleep again. That is not what we want. So, we take things beforehand.

An easy way to wake up in the morning is to have some encouragement ready for you. Either it's gym or work. It will make you wake up in the morning early to jump-start whatever you have planned. Then the mornings will be a lot more efficient for you and much more enjoyable. The first thing that we tend to do right after waking up is to check our phones. We waste 20 minutes or more just lying there doing nothing much of a task. Let's get one thing clear. It's not worth it. Wake up in the morning, get a cup of coffee, and start your day without any technology, naturally.

Once you fall into a habit, you will fall into a routine. Your life will change for the good, and you will look towards the brighter side of life. Mornings are a precious time, and 25,000 of our adulthood is the most important morning of our life. So, make sure that you make every morning out of those 25,000 mornings count. It won't be easy, but it will be worth it!